TECHNICAL REPORT

First Year Evaluation of the Caruth Police Institute at Dallas

Robert C. Davis

Sponsored by the University of North Texas with funds from the Communities Foundation of Texas

Center on Quality Policing

A RAND INFRASTRUCTURE, SAFETY, AND ENVIRONMENT CENTER

This report was sponsored by the University of North Texas at Dallas with funds from the Communities Foundation of Texas and was conducted under the auspices of the RAND Center on Quality Policing (CQP), part of the Safety and Justice Program within RAND Infrastructure, Safety, and Environment (ISE).

Library of Congress Cataloging-in-Publication Data

Davis, Robert C. (Robert Carl)
 First year evaluation of the Caruth Police Institute at Dallas / Robert C. Davis.
   p. cm.
 Includes bibliographical references.
 ISBN 978-0-8330-5059-5 (pbk. : alk. paper)
 1. Caruth Police Institute—Evaluation. 2. Police training—Texas—Dallas—Evaluation. 3. Police—Study and teaching—Texas—Dallas. I. Title.

 HV8148.D2D377 2010
 363.2'2—dc22

                                                                          2010034564

The RAND Corporation is a nonprofit institution that helps improve policy and decisionmaking through research and analysis. RAND's publications do not necessarily reflect the opinions of its research clients and sponsors.

RAND® is a registered trademark.

Published 2011 by the RAND Corporation
1776 Main Street, P.O. Box 2138, Santa Monica, CA 90407-2138
1200 South Hayes Street, Arlington, VA 22202-5050
4570 Fifth Avenue, Suite 600, Pittsburgh, PA 15213-2665
RAND URL: http://www.rand.org/
To order RAND documents or to obtain additional information, contact
Distribution Services: Telephone: (310) 451-7002;
Fax: (310) 451-6915; Email: order@rand.org

Preface

This is the first-year process-evaluation report of the W. W. Caruth Jr. Police Institute in Dallas, Texas. It analyzes the early development of the institute, assesses the extent to which strategies were implemented as planned, discusses obstacles encountered, and assesses whether the institute has lived up to initial expectations. The evaluation was funded by the University of North Texas at Dallas with funds from the Communities Foundation of Texas. It is intended for an audience of researchers and criminal-justice practitioners interested in policing issues.

The RAND Center on Quality Policing

This research was conducted under the auspices of the RAND Center on Quality Policing (CQP), part of the Safety and Justice Program within RAND Infrastructure, Safety, and Environment (ISE). The center's mission is to help guide the efforts of police agencies to improve the efficiency, effectiveness, and fairness of their operations. The center's research and analysis focus on force planning (e.g., recruitment, retention, training), performance measurement, cost-effective best practices, and use of technology, as well as issues in police-community relations.

The mission of ISE is to improve the development, operation, use, and protection of society's essential physical assets and natural resources and to enhance the related social assets of safety and security of individuals in transit and in their workplaces and communities. Safety and Justice Program research addresses occupational safety, courts and corrections, and public safety—including violence prevention, policing, substance abuse, and public integrity.

Questions or comments about this report should be sent to the author, Robert C. Davis (Robert_Davis@rand.org). Information is available online about the Safety and Justice Program (http://www.rand.org/ise/safety) and CQP (http://cqp.rand.org). Inquiries about CQP or about research projects should be sent to the following address:

Greg Ridgeway
Director, Safety and Justice Program
RAND Corporation
1776 Main Street, P.O. Box 2138
Santa Monica, CA 90407-2138
310-393-0411, x7734
Greg_Ridgeway@rand.org

Contents

Figures

Tables

Summary

In March 2009, the Dallas Police Department (DPD) began a unique partnership with two local universities, the University of North Texas (UNT) and the University of Texas at Dallas (UT Dallas). Start-up funds to create the W. W. Caruth Jr. Police Institute at Dallas (CPI) were provided by a $10 million gift from the Communities Foundation of Texas (CFT). The institute will provide training for officers at all stages of their careers and will serve as the research and problem-solving arm of the DPD, providing solutions to complex policing problems and developing effective crime-fighting strategies.

This report describes the results of a first-year process evaluation of CPI based on an evaluation design that RAND researchers prepared with funding from CFT. The design included a process evaluation of the institute's first-year operations and an impact evaluation to assess whether and how the institute is able to make the DPD more effective. The process evaluation described in this report focused on the setup of the institute. It examines the extent to which the institute is meeting its operational goals and the milestones set forth in its business plan developed for CFT. It also examines obstacles to implementation and how the institute has responded to these challenges.

In addition to gathering data for the process evaluation, we also collected data during the first year to serve as a baseline or benchmark for measuring the institute's effects in subsequent years. The results of the baseline measures of community opinion of the police, officer job satisfaction, and several other items are contained in the companion RAND document, *Measuring the Performance of the Dallas Police Department: 2008–2009 Results* (Davis, 2009).

Methods used in the process evaluation included collection of information from DPD and institute records, interviews with CPI staff, interviews with senior DPD managers, interviews with participants in CPI's inaugural course for lieutenants, course evaluations completed by participating lieutenants, and observations of CPI board of steward meetings and classes. Through the use of these multiple methods, we hoped to gain a solid understanding of the start-up challenges that the institute faced and the extent to which the institute is meeting its operational goals and milestones.

The report finds that, although the institute got off to a slow start, it assembled a well-qualified staff that created a state-of-the-art leadership class for lieutenants as its first course. The course, given in weekly modules over a period of six months, included lectures by CPI staff instructors, guest lecturers, case studies, and Friday forums that featured candid discussions between DPD chiefs and CPI staff on a variety of current topics. The class, which could be taken for UNT undergraduate or graduate credit, was well-received by participants, based on the student evaluations. Interviews with participants indicated that the course had significant team-building value: By graduation, the lieutenants had developed a common approach to leadership, a common language, and a common commitment to apply the leadership principles that they had learned to their jobs. The development of a cohort of midlevel managers who think similarly on issues is something that distinguishes CPI from other quality leadership programs.

The research and problem-solving component of the institute is also off to a solid start. The fact that the institute had to be quartered initially at DPD headquarters (because UNT Dallas did not yet have space available to house CPI) proved to be fortuitous. Institute fellows from UT Dallas have several significant research projects under way. Moreover, the institute has been receiving an increasing number of requests from members of the DPD command staff to use research to inform or evaluate DPD programs. It is unlikely that this integration of the institute would have happened as quickly or to the same extent had the institute been housed outside of DPD headquarters. The institute's research capacity is currently limited, however, by the fact that the institute has not effectively filled the position of research director. The executive director has so far acted as research director on an ad hoc basis, but this is not a tenable long-term solution because the executive director's time is being stretched increasingly thin.

Adherence of the two universities to their commitments will be key to long-term sustainability. Between the universities and the city, the four senior positions in the institute, as well as office space, should be covered once the initial four-year budget period ends. However, the fact that the research-director position has not yet been picked up as specified in the memorandum of understanding (MOU) between CFT and the university partners is cause for concern. Another cause for concern is the fact that the City of Dallas has discontinued tuition reimbursement for police officers taking academic courses. This likely will continue to have a significant impact on the proportion of officers who use CPI courses to pursue academic degrees and dampen enthusiasm for participating in CPI courses, whether on a credit or noncredit basis.

Demand for course participation from agencies in the region is building as word of the institute spreads. Opening courses to other agencies is one of the keys to sustainability: The extent to which the institute limits its scope to Dallas versus becoming a regional public-safety training center is one that institute staff, CFT, the two universities, and the City of Dallas will need to work through in the coming years.

Acknowledgments

During the course of our evaluation work, we relied heavily on DPD and CPI senior staff for information and access to staff for interviews. Throughout the project, we received excellent cooperation that made our jobs much easier than they could have been. Particular thanks are due to former DPD chief David Kunkle, deputy chief Michael Genovesi, and CPI executive director Robert Taylor. We also wish to thank the staff of CPI, DPD command staff, and the lieutenants who participated in CPI's inaugural course for their generosity in giving their time.

Special thanks are due to Jeverley R. Cook, executive director of the W. W. Caruth Jr. Foundation, and to UNT Dallas president John Price, without whose support CPI and this project would not have been possible.

Evaluation staff included Christopher Ortiz, who assisted in designing assessment instruments and interviews of DPD staff, and Rosa Maria Torres at RAND, who provided administrative support.

Abbreviations

CFT	Communities Foundation of Texas
CPI	W. W. Caruth Jr. Police Institute
DEA	Drug Enforcement Administration
DOJ	U.S. Department of Justice
DPD	Dallas Police Department
DUI	driving under the influence
FBI	Federal Bureau of Investigation
IDC	indirect cost
ILEA	Institute for Law Enforcement Administration
JHU	Johns Hopkins University
LPO	Leadership in Police Organizations
MOU	memorandum of understanding
PERF	Police Executive Research Forum
SAC	special agent in charge
SMIP	Senior Management Institute for Police
UNT	University of North Texas
UT Dallas	University of Texas at Dallas

CHAPTER ONE

Introduction

This paper reports on the first-year evaluation of the W. W. Caruth Jr. Police Institute (CPI) in Dallas. The institute was the result of an unprecedented $10 million gift from the Communities Foundation of Texas (CFT) to the Dallas Police Department (DPD). The purpose of the gift was to build the organization's long-term capacity to more effectively fight crime and respond to public concerns. CFT commissioned RAND to recommend how the DPD might spend this grant to best effect and to assist in developing a formal grant proposal to CFT based on the concept developed.

RAND researchers recommended that the best investment of the funds would be to establish CPI, a partnership that teamed the DPD with two local universities. CPI was designed to make leadership and other types of training for DPD staff an integral part of staff development and career advancement. It was also intended to partner the DPD with local academics, the business community, and national experts in developing solutions to complex policing problems and innovative solutions to preventing and deterring crime. A primary objective for CPI would be to promote Dallas as a laboratory for testing and evaluating new strategies to fight crime and respond to community needs. Figure 1.1 depicts the concept behind CPI.

As the diagram indicates, the institute has two components. One is concerned with staff-development courses at all levels within the DPD:

- At the recruit and sergeant levels, the institute will supplement current DPD training programs. For recruits, the supplement will emphasize community policing and tactical crime fighting. For sergeants, the supplemental material will stress problem solving, applying research and best practices, and understanding police culture in order to lead effectively.
- At the midlevel-manager (lieutenant) level, courses will include small-business management, strategic planning, evidence-based and problem-solving approaches to policing, CompStat processes, and theories of leadership.
- At the executive (assistant chief) level, the curriculum will incorporate courses on understanding policing within the context of other city services, comparative approaches to policing in major metropolitan departments, organizational theory and change, and futures research (understanding how the context of policing will change over the coming years).

The second component of the institute provides a forum for the DPD to solve complex management problems through discussion between police administrators, business leaders, and university scholars, bringing to bear information from national best practices. It also serves

Figure 1.1
Institute Model

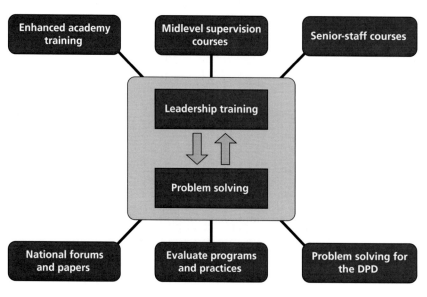

RAND *TR851-1.1*

as a laboratory, by comparing and measuring the effects of different crime-fighting approaches or community-relations campaigns. By fostering competition, the institute aims to spur division and midlevel managers to apply and test innovative solutions to policing problems and for the DPD to develop a library of effective, evidence-based practices. The overall goal of implementing and evaluating effective programs is grounded in the following discrete activities:

- Solve complex DPD problems, such as patrol deployment, with the aid of institute faculty, visiting academics and police executives, local business leaders, and executive-course class projects.
- Develop, apply, and evaluate new approaches to crime fighting and police management. Apply evaluation results to modify and improve programs and strategies utilizing the CompStat process.
- Lead in the development of sophisticated metrics to monitor trends in performance of districts and special units.
- Compare patrol districts and special units with past performance and with similar units. Disseminate results publicly for enhanced accountability.
- Promote DPD as a national center on police training and innovation. Track best practices in use of force, conducting stops, and other areas, to maintain state-of-the-art training materials. Explore new staffing, management, and leadership models. Hold forums on current policing issues.

Expected benefits of the instructional function of the leadership institute include better-trained officers better able to respond to Dallas' crime challenge and to effectively protect and serve its citizens. Officers who successfully complete leadership courses leading to college credits and advanced degrees will be better positioned for promotions, resulting in longer retention of the most-capable leaders by the Dallas Police Department. The institute also aims to enhance public safety and public confidence in the police through improved leadership and through the application of field skills learned. Finally, with the inclusion of tactical and management training courses and applications of lessons in the field, the institute would have the potential to make a quick dent in targeted crime.

About This Report

The evaluation design that RAND researchers prepared envisioned both process- and impact-evaluation methodologies. The process evaluation was intended to look at how well strategies were implemented, identify obstacles to implementation, examine how the institute responded to the obstacles, and assess whether the institute has lived up to expectations during its first year of operations. Process evaluation can be used for a number of purposes. It can assess the quality or strength of an intervention, explain why certain results are achieved, elucidate relationships between program components, and identify factors that mediate program success (Linnan and Steckler, 2002). In our case, the first-year process evaluation examines the extent to which the institute is meeting its operational goals and the milestones set forth in its business plan developed for CFT. It also examines obstacles to implementation and how the institute has responded to these challenges. This report discusses the findings from the process evaluation.

We also collected data during the first year to serve as a baseline or benchmark against which to measure how the creation of the institute affects policing in Dallas. It was anticipated in the evaluation plan that efforts to determine how CPI affects the quality of policing in Dallas would begin in the institute's second year of operation, once classes were up and running and problem-solving processes established with the DPD. The RAND plan anticipated that comparable data would be collected annually to compare with the benchmarks. The results of the baseline measures of community opinion of the police, officer job satisfaction, and several other items are contained in the companion RAND document, *Measuring the Performance of the Dallas Police Department: 2008–2009 Results* (Davis, 2009).

CHAPTER TWO

Research Methods

A memorandum of understanding (MOU) between CFT, the University of North Texas (UNT), the University of Texas at Dallas (UT Dallas), and the City of Dallas creating the institute was signed in March 2009, and the institute offered its first course in September 2009. During this period of planning and implementation, the evaluation work focused on determining whether the institute was taking the steps needed to conduct operations at a level that will produce the kind of far-reaching effects envisioned by the DPD and CFT. We have divided the process-evaluation questions into three major categories:

- management and implementation issues (how well structural challenges are being met)
  - Is the institute staffed appropriately?
  - Are physical needs of institute being met?
  - Are the partner institutions working well together?
  - Is the institute progressing toward sustainability?
- progress toward leadership development (curriculum development, integration of course-work into DPD staff development)
  - Are courses being offered on regular basis at all levels?
  - Is the curriculum innovative on the national stage?
  - Has the institute increased the number of DPD management staff getting leadership training?
  - Do attendees value courses and apply lessons to their work?
  - Has the institute worked with the DPD to develop a process for developing and cultivating future leaders?
- progress toward research and problem solving (marshaling resources for problem-solving efforts, development of evidence-based policing framework)
  - Is the DPD using the institute in the problem-solving role envisioned? Has that partnership paid concrete dividends to the DPD?
  - Is the institute generating, publishing, and using performance measures?
  - Has the institute developed a process for disseminating best practices to other departments?
  - Has the institute involved university faculty and the business community in solving large DPD problems?
  - Has the institute induced the DPD to develop an evidence-based approach to policing?
  - Is DPD management making a commitment to performance indicators?

Tables 2.1–2.3 describe the indicators that we examined in order to address each of the topics in the process evaluation.

In conducting the process evaluation, we used information from a variety of sources, including interviews with institute staff, interviews with DPD senior staff, observations of meetings of the institute's board of stewards, CPI and DPD records, literature on police leadership training, on-site observations, course evaluations, and the career paths of a cohort of officers.

Table 2.1
Management and Implementation

Question	Indicator
Is the institute staffed appropriately?	Number of staff positions filled and vacant Effectiveness of search and selection process Staff qualifications Composition of board of stewards
Are the institute's physical needs being met?	Classrooms adequate to the number of students and course needs Appropriate work space for institute staff Progress toward finding permanent space
Are the partner institutions working well together?	Relations between police chief and UNT and UT Dallas administrators Relations between city government and UNT and UT Dallas administrators Effective cooperation among members of board of stewards
Is the institute progressing toward sustainability?	Securing funding from federal or state grants or contracts Income from tuition for officers outside DPD Development of other revenue streams

Table 2.2
Leadership Development

Question	Indicator
Are courses being offered on regular basis at all levels?	Number of different courses offered Enrollment in mandatory and elective courses Number of DPD staff working on degrees Course times and modalities encourage staff participation
Is the curriculum innovative on the national stage?	Models used for course material Approach to teaching leadership Use of real-life DPD problems in class and individual projects Use of UNT and UT Dallas faculty, local businesspeople, and visiting police and academic experts in teaching roles
Has the institute increased the number of DPD management staff getting leadership training?	Increase in number of DPD staff taking leadership courses annually Increase in proportion of DPD staff who have taken a leadership course
Do attendees value courses and apply lessons to their work?	Course evaluations Pre/post course changes in knowledge Participants' application of course materials to their jobs
Has the institute worked with the DPD to develop a process for identifying and cultivating future leaders?	Procedures or guidelines for identifying potential leaders at the academy level or later

Table 2.3
Research and Problem Solving

Question	Indicator
Is the DPD using the institute in the problem-solving role envisioned? Has that partnership paid concrete dividends to the DPD?	Use of class projects to solve problems Involvement of institute and UNT and UT Dallas faculty in problem-solving efforts Involvement of visiting police executive and academic expert in problem-solving efforts Forums for regular exchange of ideas between institute and DPD staff Involvement of institute and UNT and UT Dallas faculty in problem-solving efforts
Is the institute generating, publishing, and using performance measures?	Development of set of performance indicators Regular production of indicators Public access to indicators
Has the institute developed a process for disseminating best practices to other departments?	Development of institute website and number of hits Conferences held and scheduled Publications and scope of distribution
Has the institute involved university faculty and the business community in solving large DPD problems?	Regular forums for involvement of faculty and the business community in DPD strategic planning and problem solving Specific problems in which faculty and businesspeople play a role
Has the institute induced the DPD to develop an evidence-based approach to policing?	Evaluation of new programs Evaluation of ongoing programs Translation of evaluation findings to practice
Is DPD management making a commitment to performance indicators?	Use of performance indicators in strategic planning and CompStat processes Making performance indicators available to the public

Interviews with Institute Staff

We conducted numerous interviews in person and by phone throughout the evaluation period in order to generate information about the institute's progress in each of the three domains and keep the evaluation team informed about current activities and milestones reached. Staff interviewed included the institute director, associate director for training, other instructional staff, and research staff. Topics included development of the physical capacity of the institute, relations with DPD and UNT staff, efforts to attract independent funding, progress toward developing a curriculum, use of the institute as a factor in promotion decisions, forums developed to promote the use of the institute as a problem-solving resource for the DPD, evaluations of new and existing DPD programs, and use of university faculty and business community as problem-solving resources.

Interviews with DPD Senior Staff

We conducted periodic interviews in person and by phone with the police chief, assistant chiefs for training and for research, and other senior staff to understand the institute's progress toward objectives from their perspective. The interviews, ranging from 20 to 45 minutes, covered implementation progress, the institute's effect on the DPD, and thoughts about the future of the institute. Interviews in the spring will focus on the ways in which the first lieutenant-course participants approach their jobs differently as a result of the course in which they have participated.

Observations of Meetings of the Institute Board of Stewards

We attended several meetings of the board of stewards to observe and to ask questions about decisions reached and actions taken by the board. Going forward, we will seek to conduct structured interviews annually with each board member.

Caruth Police Institute and Dallas Police Department Records

We collected information from CPI records, including the MOU specifying responsibilities of the partners, institute, the institute's business plan, staff qualifications, the content of courses, and the methods of choosing class participants, and records on the backgrounds of course participants. From the DPD, we received data on the educational attainment of staff and on the number of separations and reasons for separations for the past three years. This information will become part of the baseline data against which the institute's success will be assessed over the coming years.

Literature on Police Leadership Training

We conducted a review of literature on law-enforcement leadership training to determine best practices in the field. We also interviewed staff from several leadership training programs to fill in gaps in our understanding of what their programs included.

On-Site Observations

Each week that the institute's first course was in session, we observed the content of the classes and the interaction between instructors and class participants.

Course Evaluations

We worked with institute staff to develop course evaluations that will assess participants' satisfaction with course content and instruction and knowledge gained on specific topics. In order to assess the effects of the course, we started by examining course-evaluation forms developed by institute staff. We also collected our own assessments that included both pre- and post-course comparisons among participants, as well as comparisons between course participants and a comparison group of lieutenants who did not take the course. The measures include (a) decisionmaking ability, based on responses to hypothetical problems likely to be encountered in command positions (administered pre and post both to course participants and to nonparticipating lieutenants); (b) changes in self-assessed leadership qualities and abilities (also administered pre and post both to course participants and to nonparticipating lieutenants); (c) changes in job performance assessed by asking course participants to describe significant recent accomplishments (to be administered several months after course completion, both to participants and to nonparticipating lieutenants); and (d) perceptions of supervisors of the lieutenants who took the course of changes in course participants' approach to their assignments.

Tracking the Career Paths of a Cohort of Officers

In the evaluation plan, we said that we would select ten Dallas officers during the first year of the evaluation and track their careers over a period of years to determine how they used institute training to advance their career goals and how the institute affected their career trajectories. Since the lieutenant course was the first course offered by the institute, we decided to select the ten officers from among the participants in the inaugural course. We asked for volunteers and took the first ten that applied.

In October 2009, we interviewed the ten lieutenants about their career goals, about their initial impressions of the course, and about their thoughts on the DPD. The interviews lasted about 15 minutes and were conducted in private rooms at the conference center where the course was being held. We will document the actual course of their careers—the extent to which they take advantage of institute courses, whether they stay with the DPD, and whether they are promoted. We plan to interview each officer in this cohort during each subsequent year that the evaluation is funded. The interviews will query officers about career goals, job satisfaction, and satisfaction with progress toward their goals. The in-depth information gathered from these interviews will add a human dimension to the evaluation work describing the effects of the institute.

Information from these multiple sources has been synthesized and important lessons about the institute abstracted for this report. In drawing conclusions, we have been especially attentive to patterns that emerge from the results—that is, in findings that are corroborated by multiple sources of information. The chapters that follow describe the first-year experience of the institute and how it dealt with significant obstacles.

CHAPTER THREE

Staffing and Infrastructure

The CPI executive director, Robert Taylor, was a clear choice to head the institute. Taylor was one of the architects of the institute and chair of the criminal-justice department at UNT. His lengthy resume as a trainer and consultant to law-enforcement agencies; authorship of several popular textbooks on police administration, juvenile justice, and criminal investigation; and his extensive contacts in the law-enforcement community made him well-qualified to assume the directorship.

Getting the institute off the ground was a slow process at first. The institute involved a complex set of relationships between two universities, the City of Dallas, and CFT, making the process of drawing up an MOU a lengthy one. The process was complicated further by the fact that UNT Dallas was just in the process of becoming a separate university from UNT in Denton: While the institute was part of UNT Dallas, it initially had to rely on UNT in Denton for the ability to give college credits and degrees, as well as for payroll, computer services, grant administration, and other administrative support. Since the institute was a unique collaboration designed to marshal university resources for the benefit of the DPD, it took time to work out internal agreements and legal documents explicating the collaboration.

The DPD stepped up and offered CPI free temporary space in the police headquarters at 1200 S. Lamar Street until construction was complete for the institute's permanent home on the campus of UNT Dallas. Office equipment (desks, phones, and computers) was purchased with money from the grant. Although the space at DPD headquarters was initially intended to be temporary, the location has proven advantageous for integrating the institute into DPD operations. Institute staff have been called on to help solve everyday issues and problems, from reviewing vehicle-chase and use-of-force policies to active participation in the CompStat process. While future plans call for an office in a new building at UNT Dallas, primary offices are expected to remain at DPD headquarters.

The first staff person to assist the institute director was Jennifer Davis, project coordinator, formerly director of a health project at UNT. She handles all budgetary and compliance issues on grants, locates classroom space, and coordinates logistics for the courses. The DPD assigned Lt. Sally Lannom to the institute. She acts as liaison between CPI and the DPD command staff.

The grant proposal that funded CPI envisioned three associate directors: one for training, one for research, and one for external affairs. In June 2009, the first of these positions was filled when Richard Smith was hired as associate director in charge of training. Smith is a former assistant professor at the University of Texas at Arlington and public-safety director for Southlake, Texas.

CPI also has temporary assistance in the form of Peter Johnstone, former vice president and provost at UNT. Johnstone has an extensive background in policing, having served as an officer with the London Metropolitan Police, as well as receiving his doctorate degree in international law and administration. Johnstone assists in teaching CPI courses and develops case studies for use as teaching devices in the courses.

The other two associate director positions envisioned in the grant proposal have not been filled. The institute director says that it is unlikely that the institute will hire a director for external affairs in the foreseeable future. The need to make the initial $3.5 million CFT grant funds last for five years has required scaling back on some of the original plans. The position may not be missed, since the executive director has effectively taken on that role himself, making contacts and publicizing the institute in the policing world. The addition of a permanent law-enforcement executive-in-residence position will also help the institute to reach out and make statewide and national connections with other agencies.

John L. Worrall of UT Dallas was designated associate director for research. Worrall, well-published in the field of policing, is current editor of *Police Quarterly*. He does not draw a salary from CPI and does not get release time from his university for his involvement with CPI. UT Dallas has committed itself in the MOU to fund the research-director line, but, so far, funding has not materialized. As a result of his participation being pro bono, Worrall is only marginally involved with the institute's work. Worrall does supervise two UT Dallas Ph.D. students who are paid stipends by CPI for 20 hours per week of work. The graduate students assist in teaching courses, aid in developing criteria for selecting course participants, and conduct research projects. Worrall and the institute director did recently coauthor and submit a grant proposal to the National Institute of Justice to evaluate an "immersion" recruit-training program.

The other staff envisioned in the grant proposal included a police executive in residence and a scholar in residence. Rather than seek individuals to spend months at a time in Dallas, the institute has decided to use these positions to bring in prominent people for brief periods. Police executives are brought in for several days at a time to assist with teaching courses. For example, the first person, Darrel Stephens—former police chief of Charlotte-Mecklenburg— spent a day teaching the lieutenants' course and, the next day, participated in a several-hour candid discussion with Dallas chief David Kunkle on the experience of being a police chief. Other visiting law-enforcement executives included David B. Mitchell, former secretary of the Delaware Department of Safety and Homeland Security and of the Maryland State Police, and Gregory Allen, current chief for the City of El Paso and an expert on U.S.-Mexican border violence. Visiting academics were also used to aid in instruction, as well as conducting wider seminars for the benefit of the DPD.

The institute just announced that, upon his resignation as chief, David Kunkle will be joining the institute staff as the first police executive in residence, assuming much of the role of the associate director for external affairs on a contract basis. Kunkle also will help with developing and teaching institute courses.

The institute recruited members for a board of stewards that includes staff of the Dallas city manager's office, UNT and UT Dallas, the DPD, CFT, Dallas Crime Watch, and local representatives of the Drug Enforcement Administration (DEA) and the Federal Bureau of Investigation (FBI). The board meets semiannually and met for the first time in June 2009 and again in December 2009. The first meeting served to introduce the board to the institute. At the second meeting, CPI staff gave a progress report on the institute objectives. So far, the new board does not appear to have taken an active role in setting objectives or policy for the institute, but it is still too early to tell how active the board or individual members are likely to be.

Finally, there are plans to bring in people from the business community to conduct seminars for the benefit of the DPD. Contacts have been made with Southwest Airlines, American Airlines, Burlington Northern Santa Fe Railway, City Center Security (Bass Companies in Fort Worth), Frito-Lay, and Texas Instruments to assist in this venture. The hope is that DPD deputy chiefs will be matched with business leaders who will serve as coaches and mentors.

CHAPTER FOUR

Institute Courses: Developing Future Dallas Police Department Leaders

As the demands on law-enforcement agencies have grown and technology becomes increasingly complex, experts have come to recognize the importance of good police leadership (see, e.g., International Association of Chiefs of Police, 1999). There are good programs in the United States for training leaders in law enforcement, including the Senior Management Institute for Police (SMIP) (run jointly by the John F. Kennedy School of Government at Harvard and the Police Executive Research Forum, or PERF) and the FBI's National Academy, among others. There are also significant drawbacks to these programs, including cost and significant time away from the job in a residential program. Consequently, agencies—including the DPD—tend to send only a few of their top administrators to these programs.

The concept behind CPI is very different from that of other programs that train police leaders. Most obviously, the classes are local, so participants do not need to be away from home and the department does not have to pay for transportation, hotel, and per diem costs associated with residential programs. Moreover, CPI courses are conducted in blocks of one week per month: Even though the total number of class hours is enough to qualify for nine graduate credits or 15 undergraduate credits, participants are not away from the job for extended periods of time.

But, more fundamentally, CPI is a wholly new approach to leadership training. It looks at learning as a career-long process: CPI is involved in the DPD's training all the way from the recruit stage to the level of senior management. It offers officers continuous chances to increase their effectiveness on the job, to earn undergraduate and advanced degrees, and to expand their opportunities for advancement at all stages of their careers. CPI is also unique in that cohorts of officers from particular ranks go through the program together. Instead of developing a few trained individuals as leaders, CPI courses graduate classes of several dozen officers who have shared experiences over a period of six-week sessions. There is a chance to develop group cohesion and to form professional relationships that will last throughout officers' careers. The cohorts of officers graduating from CPI courses using the same language and same ways of thinking about policing problems have the potential to quickly and significantly change the culture of the department.

In the spring of 2009, CPI staff began a careful process of planning the courses to be offered through the institute. They did a scan of practice to determine the scope of supervision and management courses that were being offered across the country for law-enforcement personnel. They examined the topics and content of major textbooks on police supervision, management, and administration. They also examined academic literature on innovative training techniques, current trends in police management training, and adult learning strategies.

Course planning began in earnest with focus groups led by Eric J. Fritsch, professor and associate chair of the Department of Criminal Justice at UNT in Denton. The focus groups, which included both command staff and midlevel supervisors, asked participants for their views on what kinds of training were needed to perform their jobs most effectively and on the format and delivery options for courses. The sergeants' focus group indicated that the most-critical needs were in the areas of leading and motivating diverse personnel, handling discipline and performance evaluations, liability issues, managing change, and keeping abreast of evidence-based practices. For lieutenants, the needs expressed centered on mentoring and career development, grant writing, project management, budgeting, interagency cooperation, decisionmaking, and research methods for police managers.

Fritsch also conducted a *scan of practice*, contacting some of the best police leadership training programs in the country, including those run by the International Association of Chiefs of Police and PERF, to gain a detailed understanding of how their leadership programs were structured. CPI's director made connections early on with administrators of the police executive leadership program at Johns Hopkins University (JHU) in Columbia, Maryland. So far, the connection has brought staff from JHU in to teach portions of courses at CPI. CPI and JHU are in the process of drawing up an MOU that will formalize ongoing faculty exchange and other forms of cooperation. In the future, this relationship may also offer an avenue to connect DPD supervisors with their counterparts from other agencies who are enrolled in the JHU program.

The curriculum for the lieutenants' course was a synthesis of the local needs assessed in the focus groups, national best practices in leadership training, and the considerable experience of CPI's executive director and the associate director for training.

Lieutenants' Course

The first course offered through the institute was a leadership class for lieutenants, with the broad objective to identify and prepare the next generation of leaders for the Dallas Police Department. This was a sound decision, as findings from our needs assessment demonstrated that lieutenants in the DPD are a traditionally undertrained group that has had only limited training opportunities available to them.

About 80 of the DPD's 120 lieutenants attended the introductory sessions. Lieutenants who decided to apply were asked to provide a description of how the course would fit into their career goals. The selection process was to have been based on these personal statements, time in rank, performance evaluations, education, letters of recommendation, and disciplinary history, as well as ethnic and gender diversity. As it turned out, 24 of the 120 lieutenants applied for the 26 slots, so all were accepted. The fact that more lieutenants did not apply for the course may have been a function of the newness of the institute, but it is likely also related to the city's withdrawal of tuition reimbursement for police officers taking college courses—a cost-saving move that unfortunately occurred just before the institute opened its doors.

Lacking adequate class space either at the DPD or UNT Dallas, the class was held in a conference room at a local arboretum. While the space is attractive, the cost for the ten-week session is $4,000–5,000 per week for space and food. However, the institute recently secured a commitment from the Meadows Foundation to host future courses and provide lunches for participants.

The 240-hour course, which began in October, provided nine hours of graduate or 15 hours of undergraduate credit. However, few of the participants took the course for college credit, likely again due to the fact that the city no longer reimburses officers who take college courses. The first CPI class convened on September 14, 2009. Each module began with lectures by institute staff on the first two days based on assigned readings. On the third day, Johnstone introduced a case study customized from *Harvard Business Review*. On the fourth day, a guest lecturer took over the class. The lecturers were nationally recognized experts in policing, including both police leaders and academics. The final day included a discussion between the guest lecturer and a high-ranking member of the DPD, moderated by the institute director.

The six course modules are built on the results of the focus groups held by Eric Fritsch. Each module is one week in length, and one module was scheduled monthly through February 2010. Approximately one-third of the 240 classroom hours were devoted to traditional lecture methodology. Key themes explored during this course included leadership practices, organizational structure and impediments, organizational change, performance evaluation, and human resources and diversity issues. Throughout all coursework, continued emphasis was placed on the role of leadership within organizations. For example, the first module consisted of a general discussion about police leadership and what it entails. This was then followed by a block on leadership and organizational development and a block on best practices in organizational leadership. Lecturers included university professors, external police executives, and internal command staff. This blend provided students with a broad-based understanding of the issues under examination and allowed for candid discussions, emphasizing issues that currently exist within the DPD.

Between each set of modules, students were expected to complete a demanding reading list, which included several seminal works in leadership and police studies. Many of these texts are utilized in competing police leadership courses. Examples included Malcolm Gladwell's (2000) *The Tipping Point* and Kouzes and Posner's (1987) *The Leadership Challenge*. The extent and depth of the reading material were substantial. At the conclusion of the course, the lieutenant-students were exposed to a wide breadth of leadership material.

Each weeklong module was capped off by a case study. The case studies expanded on issues raised in class using a problem-solving approach. The case studies were produced by Harvard Business School, and the instruction was led by a senior UNT faculty member. Case studies have gained increased popularity in law-enforcement training, being most notably utilized by the SMIP program created by PERF in conjunction with faculty from Harvard Kennedy School. Students at CPI were required to work both in groups and independently to provide real-world solutions to the issues raised in the case study. Discussions were led by the senior faculty member, and students were encouraged to provide feedback recommending action. At the conclusion, students submitted a written document outlining the issues raised in the case study and their proposed solution to the problem. This, in turn, was graded and returned to the students. The conversations during the case studies were spirited. According to the instructor, a marked increase in performance in terms of writing quality and progressive problem solving was noted in the case studies from one session to the next. The instructor observed that, by the end of the course, the CPI lieutenants were thinking and writing on an advanced postgraduate level.

The topics and visiting faculty for the six sessions of the lieutenants' course included the following:

- "Defining Police Leadership," September 14–18, 2009: Darrel Stephens, former chief from Charlotte-Mecklenburg, North Carolina, and former president of PERF, presented material on the role of chief of police in a major city.
- "Organizational Strategies and Change," October 26–30, 2009: Michael J. Heidingsfield, current assistant sergeant at arms for the U.S. Senate and former police chief from Scottsdale, Arizona, discussed his two-year experience as a consultant attempting to change the Baghdad, Iraq, police department.
- "Diversity and Promotional Systems," November 16–20, 2009: Charles R. "Mike" Swanson, former director of the Carl Vinson Institute of Government at the University of Georgia, presented material on promotion systems.
- "Policing Styles and Philosophies," December 14–18, 2009: John Liederbach, professor at Bowling Green State University in Ohio, and Sheldon Greenberg, director of the Police Executive Leadership Program at JHU, presented extensive discussion on the police subculture, corruption, ethics, and the role of police.
- "Decision-Making and Political Management," January 19–22, 2010: Lowell Cannaday, former chief of the Irving, Texas, police department, and his wife, Rose Cannaday, current Irving city council member, discussed politics in the police process. They also provide interesting discussion into "making a relationship work" while serving as the top police executive.
- "Contemporary Issues: Police Response to Violence Stemming from the U.S.-Mexican Border," February 16–19, 2010: Robert E. Casey, Jr., special agent in charge (SAC) of the Dallas FBI field office, and Michael Lee, SAC of the Secret Service's Dallas field office, provided in-depth briefings. Gregory Allen and Peter F. Pacillas of the El Paso Police Department provided keen insight into violence on the border.

The Experience of Participants in the Lieutenants' Course

Participants in the lieutenants' course were asked to fill out evaluation forms after each week's class was concluded. The results were very positive. Participants agreed or strongly agreed that the class improved their understanding of leadership concepts, that the class setting was conducive to learning, that the Friday morning panels were useful, that there was sufficient time for discussion, that reading materials were relevant, that the discussions about the case studies were effective, and that the class objectives were clearly defined (see Figure 4.1). The only evaluation item with which students did not agree was whether the work given outside of class was excessive: Here, the rating did not indicate clear agreement or disagreement.

RAND staff conducted semistructured interviews with ten of the lieutenants' course participants midway through the course. The interviews revealed that CPI staff were very enthusiastic about the initial sessions of the lieutenants' course. They were especially impressed by the final day in the first week's session, when Stephens and Kunkle shared personal thoughts on the job of police chief. (In fact, several of the lieutenants said that this session had given them pause in considering whether or not they would ever like to be a chief themselves.)

The interviews indicated that participants liked the course design and structure and that they thought that the mix of learning sources was a positive aspect of the training. Several students recounted gaining valuable information from the outside police executives, while others believed that the candid interface with their own chief was the most positive aspect of the class. The use of the case-study methodology was also well received. The vast majority of lieutenants interviewed had never experienced a case-study learning method prior to this course, but

Figure 4.1
Student Evaluations of Lieutenants' Course

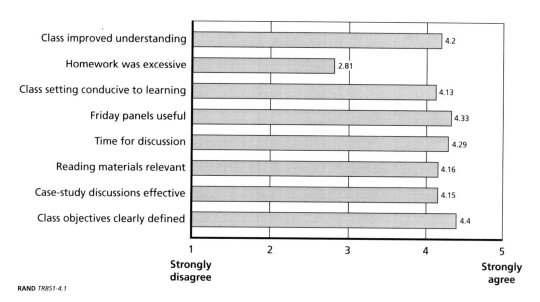

all seemed to appreciate its value. The lieutenants' least favorite aspect of the course was the amount of work required outside the classroom. Many thought that the reading was too extensive and required too much time to complete.

The decision not to open up the initial lieutenants' course to officers outside Dallas was a sound one. Course instructors reported—and course participants reinforced this during our interviews—that the course has team-building value. Several of the ten course participants whom we interviewed talked about developing a greater appreciation of their peers and a developing sense of solidarity within the class. The building sense of solidarity may be particularly strong in this first class because the participants were the first to volunteer for this program and because the lieutenants in the course were young and relatively new to their positions (most have been promoted within the past three years).

The development of a cohort of midlevel managers who think similarly on issues is likely to bring pressure on the DPD administration to adopt changes that will make decisions about strategy, assignments, and promotions more rational, egalitarian, and transparent. The lieutenants with whom we spoke had a sense of enthusiasm about their jobs and a strong desire to participate in improving the department. They were eager to put the leadership principles they were learning in the course to work on the job. However, four saw some deputy and assistant DPD chiefs as apprehensive about expectations for greater participation in decisions among the newly energized cohort of lieutenants completing the course. A couple of the lieutenants with whom we spoke saw this as a critical test for the institute: If institute graduates can put into practice the principles they learned in the course, the institute will come to be seen as a positive force for change and officers will seek to participate in its courses. But, if it is seen that top DPD leadership does not accept the principles taught by CPI, the institute will come to be seen as irrelevant. One lieutenant expressed the need for a change in the DPD culture and hoped that the course would create a critical mass of midlevel managers who share a common language and common vision for the department.

RAND has also conducted baseline assessments that include measures of leadership skills and decisionmaking abilities for course participants and for a group of lieutenants who did not take the course. Under a new grant from CFT, RAND staff will add significant components to the assessment of the lieutenants' course. These will include postcourse measures of leadership skills and decisionmaking abilities for course participants and for a group of lieutenants who did not take the course. We will also conduct structured interviews with course participants and their supervisors to learn how course participation has affected the lieutenants' approach to their jobs.

Other Courses for Dallas Police Department Officers

The institute also planned to offer a course for assistant chiefs. The plan was to hold it in two-hour sessions once per week following CompStat meetings and to bring in leaders from the business community to conduct the seminars. CPI's director made a pitch for the class after a weekly CompStat meeting, but just one of the 30 assistant chiefs expressed interest, so the idea was temporarily shelved. The institute director speculates that the lack of interest may have stemmed from recent cuts in civilian staff that have added significantly to the workload of uniformed administrators and from the city's withdrawal of tuition reimbursement for police officers taking college courses. He expects to work with the incoming police chief to host an executive retreat for assistant chiefs to ease the transition. In addition, he hopes to build a mentoring program for the deputy chiefs, pairing DPD chiefs with leaders in the local academic and business communities.

The next executive-development module is a supervisory course for sergeants. Institute staff are now developing the selection process to determine which of the DPD's 400 sergeants will be chosen for the first class. The process will be based on an objective scoring system, with points given for college degrees, less tenure, good performance evaluations, positive recommendations from supervisors, and a clean internal-affairs record. They are also working on a survey that will query sergeants about what they would like to see included in the course. The course will incorporate state Texas Commission on Law Enforcement Officer Standards and Education training requirements, the chief's in-service training, and a more conceptual component developed by CPI.

In December, the institute jointly sponsored a one-day workshop on managing police liability with the Institute for Law Enforcement Administration (ILEA) in Plano. The workshop, which focused on the DPD chief's controversial policy on police chases and emergency vehicle operations, was open to agencies in Texas as well as in neighboring states. Institute staff are exploring future joint programs with ILEA, including midlevel management courses for smaller departments in the greater Dallas area. The partnership makes sense because ILEA is one of two state organizations that provided training to senior law-enforcement personnel prior to the founding of CPI. (The other is the Law Enforcement Management Institute of Texas, which provides training mainly to personnel of small law-enforcement agencies.) The fact that the CPI director sits on the ILEA board should facilitate coordination of efforts between CPI and ILEA.

Institute staff have integrated CPI courses with the programs and course offerings at both UNT and UT Dallas. Participants in the lieutenants' course can currently work toward an undergraduate or graduate degree from UNT in Denton or a Ph.D. from UT Dallas. Institute staff are also working toward establishing a master's degree in police leadership from UNT Dallas and a blended graduate degree with the new UNT Dallas law school beginning in the fall of 2012.

Still to be determined is how taking courses will be incorporated into the promotion process. It is a thorny issue in any event, given union pressure, considerations of seniority and diversity that enter into promotion decisions, and willingness of institute staff to disclose class performance information to DPD administrators. It will be important to observe how the new police chief will use the institute as a tool to promote staff development and retention.

Staff Educational Levels and Retention

Part of the original intent in creating the institute was to generate a better-educated police force and one that is able to retain officers for longer tenures. We hope to track changes in educational level and staff retention in the upcoming years. For now, we have put together baseline data on these indicators.

Table 4.1 displays educational attainment of DPD staff at various ranks. The table indicates that most DPD staff at the rank of corporal and above have college degrees, varying from 52 percent of corporals to 92 percent of chiefs. At lesser ranks, a minority of staff hold college degrees: Forty-three percent of officers have bachelor's degrees, as do 38 percent of officer trainees. Advanced degrees are held by 32 percent of chiefs and 14 percnt of lieutenants. Advanced degrees are extremely rare below the rank of lieutenant.

Table 4.2 presents DPD separations by year and reason. The table indicates that separations show a downward trend over the five-year period for ranks of officer and above. However, separations among trainees show an opposing trend, with separations increasing over time. Both trends in separations are in the category of voluntary separations. That is, more staff at the trainee level have quit in more-recent years, while fewer staff at the rank of officer and above have resigned. Involuntary separations have remained relatively constant over time within all ranks.

Table 4.1
College Degrees Among Dallas Police Department Sworn Staff

	None		Bachelor's		Master's		Doctorate		Total	
Rank	%	n	%	n	%	n	%	n	%	n
Chief or captain	8	2	60	15	32	8	—	0	100	25
Lieutenant	20	22	66	71	14	15	—	0	100	108
Sergeant	36	155	62	267	3	12	—	0	100	434
Corporal	48	696	51	736	1	14	<1	2	100	1,448
Officer	57	604	42	445	<1	3	—	0	100	1,052
Officer trainee	62	337	37	202	<1	2	<1	1	100	542

Table 4.2
Dallas Police Department Separations, by Year and Reason

Position	Retirement, Disability, or Death	Voluntary Separation	Involuntary Separation	Total Separations
Apprentice, trainee, or probationary officer				
2004	0	25	8	33
2005	0	27	1	28
2006	0	42	11	53
2007	0	52	10	62
2008	1	61	9	71
Officer				
2004	4	25	7	36
2005	4	22	3	29
2006	6	18	13	37
2007	3	16	3	22
2008	9	7	5	21
Corporal or senior corporal				
2004	42	9	2	53
2005	45	4	2	51
2006	45	2	3	50
2007	43	7	2	52
2008	37	2	3	42
Sergeant				
2004	15	2	0	17
2005	13	0	1	14
2006	23	0	1	24
2007	18	0	1	19
2008	12	0	0	12
Lieutenant				
2004	4	0	0	4
2005	4	0	0	4
2006	5	0	0	5
2007	4	0	1	5
2008	7	0	0	7

Table 4.2—Continued

Position	Retirement, Disability, or Death	Voluntary Separation	Involuntary Separation	Total Separations
Captain or chief				
2004	4	0	0	4
2005	0	0	0	0
2006	2	0	1	3
2007	1	0	0	1
2008	2	0	0	2
Total				
2004	69	61	17	147
2005	66	53	7	126
2006	81	62	29	172
2007	69	75	17	161
2008	68	70	17	155

SOURCE: DPD data.

CHAPTER FIVE

Research and Problem Solving: Introducing Evidence-Based Practice into Dallas Policing

A report several years ago by the National Research Council pointed out large gaps in the body of policing research (Skogan and Frydl, 2004). Moreover, Bayley (1998) argues that, despite the volume of studies, policing research has not produced broad operational changes in the way that law enforcement is done. Bradley and Nixon (2009) attribute this gap to problems with different models of policing research, which they divide into research generated by police-agency staff and critical, academic, or policy research. Researchers based within police agencies are likely to best understand the context and workings of police agencies. But their work is likely to consist mainly of using simple and less-than-optimum research methods to develop quick solutions to urgent problems. Moreover, there is a temptation to bend results in order to curry political favor with the chief. On the other hand, academic research has the virtue of being independent, but the results may be too theoretical or too long term to be of practical use to police administrators. Moreover, the differences in cultures and language between academics and police practitioners make meaningful exchange difficult (Shaftoe, 2004; Brown and Waters, 1993).

CPI represents a new model of conducting research on policing issues: one based on a partnership between academic researchers and a police agency. By bringing researchers physically into the DPD, CPI encourages researchers to learn about the police culture firsthand. At the same time, the proximity of researchers at DPD headquarters encourages police administrators to use institute staff to conduct studies, both small and large, that promote the adoption of evidence-based practices in DPD work. Still, the fact that the institute is formally a part of UNT or UT Dallas allows researchers to maintain a degree of independence in their findings and interpretations of study results.

In the CFT grant proposal, the research and problem-solving component of CPI is articulated in nearly as much detail as the staff-development component. The proposal indicates that the institute will include "class projects that analyze and propose solutions to current problems facing the department," promote regular meetings between institute faculty and DPD administrators to "analyze current practices and make suggestions for improving effectiveness," "enlist the help of senior [business] executives in providing seminars and providing advice on improving DPD operations," and, through the visiting-scholar and executive-in-residence programs, "provide the DPD with the best national expertise on policing issues." The proposal states that the institute will conduct evaluations of current DPD practices and programs, with the results used by the DPD to improve programs and published in professional journals. The proposal further indicates that the institute will, in coordination with RAND, develop and implement a set of "sophisticated performance metrics" that will be used by the DPD to improve its effectiveness and shared with citizens through the DPD website. Finally, the proposal states that the institute will serve a repository and distributor of best practices in policing through conferences and written outlets.

A year into operations, the institute has begun to integrate itself into the decisionmaking process of the DPD command staff. The executive director regularly meets with the Dallas chief and attends command staff meetings. Two UT Dallas Ph.D. students are conducting significant research projects for the DPD. One project is examining patrol strategies to reduce crime. It is using longitudinal data to examine relationships between crime rates and administrative directives (e.g., staffing patterns, overtime, response time, activity), officer-initiated behaviors (e.g., arrests, self-initiated investigations), and policing practices (e.g., foot patrol, hotspot policing, saturation patrol). Another project is evaluating a diversion program operated by the DPD's Youth Services Section. The program provides offenders with the opportunity for a second chance by providing services to them and their families. Still another institute project is conducting ethnographic research with the DPD's gang unit to understand how gang affiliates are policed compared to non–gang-affiliated suspects.

In addition to these longer-term projects, DPD command staff have begun to call on the institute to provide information to help them in determining agency strategy and making operational decisions. Some recent examples include the following:

- an assessment of a new Breathalyzer™ law for stops for suspected driving under the influence (DUI)
- an experiment evaluating simultaneous versus sequential viewing of suspect photos
- matching DNA and fingerprint data acquired from prostitutes with forensic evidence gathered from crime scenes
- providing training for Dallas' critical-incident team.

The institute has also had significant involvement in research and consulting projects regionally, statewide, and beyond. The institute houses the Reduce Auto Theft in Texas project designed to reduce vehicle crime in Texas by raising awareness about vehicle theft and burglary and by promoting practical steps to prevent auto crime. Institute staff expect that the project, which is also responsible for training statewide auto-theft task forces, will generate more than $500,000 in revenue by the end of 2010. The institute has also partnered with RAND on a project for the Bureau of Justice Assistance that is identifying international best practice in law enforcement.

The institute director has been very active in consulting with other Texas law-enforcement agencies. For the City of El Paso Police Department, he has conducted evaluations of academy training and internal-affairs policies and developed a fusion center. He also assisted in conducting departmental assessments and patrol-allocation studies for the McKinney Police Department, Rowlett Police Department, and North Richland Hills Police Department. The associate director for training has conducted retreats and staff briefings for the North Texas High Intensity Drug Trafficking Area and the City of Irving. While this is not technically CPI work, the income provided through his consulting work does flow into institute coffers. Moreover, the work has helped to promote and publicize the institute's name across the state of Texas.

The institute is also beginning to establish itself nationally. It was the topic of an article in a recent newsletter of the U.S. Department of Justice (DOJ) Office of Community Oriented Policing Services, of an upcoming article in *Police Chief* magazine, and of an upcoming panel at the annual conference of the International Association of Chiefs of Police. The institute director is also one of a select group of experts involved in a police leadership forum at the John Jay College of Criminal Justice.

The research and problem-solving component of the institute is off to a good start. The challenge going forward will be to identify ways to coordinate and promote this aspect of the institute that do not involve the executive director. The demand, both locally and beyond Dallas, is there; it is now a question of whether the institute can find a way to hire a research director so that the executive director is not stretched too thinly. If this happens, the vision of the institute as a vehicle for program evaluation and solving complex policing problems will be achievable.

CHAPTER SIX

Dallas Police Department Senior Staff's Views About the Caruth Police Institute

To understand the perspective of DPD administrators about the institute, we interviewed the police chief and five deputy and assistant chiefs. (The latter were interviewed as a group.) We asked the chiefs what they thought of the concept behind the institute, about the material covered in the lieutenants' course, about whether they thought that CPI courses would factor into promotion decisions, and about whether they believed that CPI would act as a force to change the DPD and the way that policing is done in Dallas.

As a group, the chiefs thought that the concept behind the institute was a sound one. They each believed in the value of leadership training and felt that opportunities for DPD managers had always been limited—even more so since the start of the recession. They saw a local leadership training capability as a way to offer training to a wide set of DPD managers without the large price tag associated with high-quality leadership training courses. The chiefs expected that, as funds allowed, the department would continue to send small numbers of senior administrators to remote training programs as well so that they could have a chance to interact and exchange ideas with peers from other agencies.

The chiefs noted that the institute staff had sought their input into the lieutenants' course curriculum and that one of the DPD lieutenants had played a large role in developing the course curriculum. They believed that leadership courses ought to teach participants "how to think, not what to think." That is, they thought that it was important to teach how to see an issue from all sides and where to go to find information necessary to solving problems. They said that the feedback they had been getting from course participants who worked with them was that the lieutenants' course fit this description. The course was thought to be demanding and the participants intellectually pushed. In fact, one chief said that it was challenging to the point that course preparation sometimes interfered with participants' job responsibilities.

The chiefs noted that the lieutenants especially liked the fact that a different guest lecturer was brought in for each segment of the course. Course participants saw the guest lecturers as providing fresh ways of thinking about issues and new perspectives on different aspects of policing, ranging from personnel decisions to police liability issues. Several of the chiefs had sat in on the Friday sessions in which the guest lecturer and a DPD chief had candid conversations about organizational issues and policing philosophies. They were impressed by the candor of the discussions.

The consensus among the chiefs whom we interviewed was that limiting the initial courses to Dallas personnel was a good decision. The course was seen as a vehicle for the relatively small group of lieutenants to get to know one another and develop a sense of group cohesion. Eventually, opening courses to officers outside Dallas was seen as acceptable as long as enrollment was limited to urban agencies with problems similar to those faced by the DPD.

The chiefs were not sure how CPI participation might factor into the promotion process. One remarked, "The chief is going to promote who he needs to when the need arises." But they also noted that the department ought to move toward making education a factor in promotion decisions and use CPI as a tool to encourage midlevel managers to pursue advanced degrees. One noted that, de facto, course participation will be considered at promotion time: "If you don't go for it, what message are you sending?" Kunkle noted that performance in CPI classes could become one of a variety of factors considered in promotions. However, that would require that institute staff provide the DPD with feedback on class performance, something that could prove controversial with some course participants.

The chiefs were not sure whether or how CPI course participation would affect the DPD. Noting that (at the time that the interviews were conducted) the first course was only in its second week, they thought that it was too early to tell whether the course graduates would act as a potent force for change in the DPD.

Shortly before Kunkle's departure, we asked the chief how he thought that his leaving would affect the institute that he was instrumental in creating. His response was that he believed that whomever was chosen as the new chief would lend strong support to the institute and recognize it as a valuable resource. He indicated that maintaining the institute within the DPD headquarters and direct access to the new chief were critical factors for future success. The chief felt that the institute director was really the key to its success. He expressed strong support for the job that the director has done, and he argued that the director's demonstrated commitment to keeping the DPD's interests paramount was crucial to the continued success of CPI.

CHAPTER SEVEN

Sustainability

The MOU signed with CFT gave UNT $3.5 million of the original $10 million gift to support the first four years of operation.[1] The remainder of the money was placed into a quasi-endowment, with earnings from the corpus to be used to support institute operations.

The MOU offers a partial path toward institutionalization. UNT Dallas is tasked with picking up the executive-director and associate-director-for-training lines at the end of 5.66 years. The city is tasked with providing a police lieutenant to fill the position of associate director for external affairs, and UT Dallas is tasked with picking up the associate-director-for-research line immediately. Between the entities, all four senior positions at the institute are funded in perpetuity. With the addition of the office space provided gratis by the DPD, the institute should be well positioned for sustainability.

The DPD provided the lieutenant it had pledged immediately, well ahead of the 2013 scheduled date. However, the fact that UT Dallas has not yet stepped up to provide a full-time research director raises concerns not only about the institute's present capabilities to realize the potential of its research component but also about its long-term sustainability.

An important part of the sustainability plan for CPI is for the institute to bring in cash through opening courses to officers outside Dallas or to bring in grant funds. The institute director has had several discussions with larger police departments (e.g., Dallas Area Rapid Transit Police, Dallas County Sheriff's Department, Arlington Police Department) regarding potential participation in future courses. These departments would send a limited number of officers and pay tuition to CPI. The director also plans to open courses to law-enforcement officers from outside Dallas once the course offerings and curricula are fully developed. He plans to solicit participants from El Paso and other large cities in Texas, as well as major cities around the country. He expects to collect $5,000 in tuition from each participant outside Dallas.

The institute director is also involved with a private company (Critical Information Network, or CiNet, in Carrollton, Texas) currently providing courses to the Federal Law Enforcement Training Center in Glynco, Georgia, through a federal grant. Future plans include joint development of a web-based law-enforcement training curriculum that would support courses at CPI.

While CPI needs to go after grant funds as part of a sustainability plan, it has had to deal with several obstacles. The original plan was for the associate director for research to spearhead grant-proposal efforts. However, with only minimal services being donated pro bono for this

---

[1] For institute operations, $9.5 million was available. The remainder of the $10 million was given to RAND to conduct the needs assessment and develop a concept for spending the funds.

position by UT Dallas, it is not clear how the institute will find the labor to write proposals that will enable it to compete for federal and other grants.

Another obstacle to CPI bringing in grant funds is that, as part of UNT, it is not eligible to compete for state contracts. There is a way around this, if CPI created a separate nonprofit entity, but, so far, UNT has not wanted to pursue this path. As stated earlier, the institute director has received two grants from the state for a total of $494,000 for motor-vehicle theft prevention. CPI received $50,000 on the subcontract from RAND mentioned earlier for the Bureau of Justice Assistance project to identify best international practices in policing. On these grants and the CFT award, the institute had to negotiate with UNT to get a reduction in indirect costs (IDC) taken out of the grants by the university, since CPI gets little in the way of university support (e.g., space, utilities, furniture, secretarial services). After some struggle, the university settled for an IDC rate of 14 percent.

Last summer, the institute had a unique opportunity to apply for state matching funds through the Tier One Research Initiative Program. Had the institute been able to apply, the potential funds of up to $6 million would have made the institute self-sufficient and sustainable forever. However, UNT officials determined that CPI could not seek this funding because only state-designated research universities could apply and CPI was technically was not part of UNT in Denton (UNT Dallas does not yet qualify as a research university). A current state ballot initiative could provide another chance at substantial matching funds if the institute can negotiate a way to apply for the funds through its second partner university, UT Dallas. That would involve a significant shift in CPI stewardship, giving UT Dallas a much larger role in the operations of the institute.

CHAPTER EIGHT

Progress Toward Goals and Objectives: A Caruth Police Institute Report Card

One of the first things that UNT was required to do for CFT was to develop a business plan. Included in the business plan was a set of goals and objectives for the institute. In this chapter, we describe progress that CPI has made in meeting these goals.

Twenty-nine of the 34 objectives listed in the business plan have expected completion dates that had expired at the time that this report was drafted. Of these 29, 17 have been completed, six have been partially completed, and six remain to be done. Among the most significant goals that have been attained are the following:

- filling most of the institute staff positions with well-qualified candidates
- working out agreements that allow course participants to complete undergraduate or graduate credits for CPI courses
- developing and conducting the institute's first course for lieutenants, including prominent guest lecturers
- provide consulting services to regional law-enforcement and criminal-justice agencies.

Three of the six incomplete items are related to the research and problem-solving component of the institute. They include hiring a research director (goal 1, objective 2; see Table 8.1 for a list of all goals and objectives and their current status), developing a major research project on victimization or crime prevention (goal 3, objective 4), and providing a venue to host international police delegates showcasing best practices within the DPD (goal 5, objective 3). Two are concerned with revamping the DPD's recruitment and retention program (goal 2, objective 8, and goal 3, objective 2) and are not considered priorities in a time when few new positions are available each year and other employment options for DPD officers are less available. The remaining incomplete item is evaluating the DPD academy training programs (goal 2, objective 4).

Overall, the institute has achieved a surprising amount given the substantial delays in start-up that it experienced. If it can come up with a plan to fill the position of research director, it seems likely that nearly all stated objectives can be completed by the end of 2010.

Table 8.1
Goals, Objectives, and Status

Goal or Objective	Status	Notes
Goal I: Provide and develop CPI with the organizational capacity and administrative means to carry out all programming related to achieving the CPI mission.		
Objective 1: Immediately commence work via an agreement with the RAND Corporation providing external independent third-party evaluation of CPI's effectiveness.	C	An MOU was signed between UNT and RAND in November 2008 for the first-year evaluation of CPI. Future evaluation work is being discussed.
Objective 2: Appoint an associate director of research in coordination with UT Dallas by March 1, 2009.	I	John Worrall has acted as the research director for CPI. However, the position is not supported either by UT Dallas, as was intended, or by CPI. As a result, the research/problem-solving potential envisioned in the creation of CPI has been only minimally realized.
Objective 3: Hire an associate director of training and education by July 1, 2009.	C	Rick Smith was hired as training director in the spring of 2009 and has been instrumental in developing curriculum for the institute.
Objective 4: Hire an associate director of external affairs by February 2010.	C	David Kunkle has been hired to serve both as associate director of external affairs and as police executive in residence. He is working with the private sector to develop mentor programs and with regional law-enforcement agencies to recruit outside participants in the next lieutenant class.
Objective 5: Select members and set the first meeting of the board of stewards for May 30, 2009.	C	The board was chosen and met for the first time in July 2009.
Objective 6: Sponsor a CPI open house by June 15, 2009.	C	An open house was held in August, with members of the DPD, area police chiefs, members of the board of stewards, local media, and leaders from the business community in attendance.
Goal II: Identify, help select, and train a new generation of DPD leaders by providing state-of-the-art professional development and leadership training.		
Objective 1: Review police training institutes and conduct needs assessment for the midlevel-management and supervisory courses by April 30, 2009.	C	Eric Fritsch contacted major law-enforcement training programs to gather ideas for curriculum and teaching methods. He held focus groups in the spring at the DPD to explain the institute and gather course ideas.
Objective 2: Develop curricula for midlevel-management and supervisory courses by June 2009.	C	Institute staff completed a curriculum for both programs.
Objective 3: Identify at least 15 candidates for midlevel-management training and 30 candidates for supervisory training at the DPD by July 2009.	C	Twenty-four candidates for the lieutenants' course were screened and selected during August. Selection for the first sergeants' course was recently completed.
Objective 4: Meet with academy command staff and develop a plan to evaluate current in-service training and leadership courses by August 2009.	I	Not yet completed
Objective 5: Integrate CPI leadership training courses into the academic curriculum offered at UNT Dallas Campus and UT Dallas by August 2009.	C	CPI has worked out an agreement with UNT in Denton that will give 9 hours graduate credit or 12 hours undergraduate credit for participants in the lieutenants' course interested in earning college credit. In two years, participants will be able to earn undergraduate credit at UNT Dallas.
Objective 6: Offer the first supervisory training course through CPI for the DPD by August 31, 2009.	C	The first course for sergeants recently got under way.

Table 8.1—Continued

Goal or Objective	Status	Notes
Objective 7: Implement one midlevel-management course for DPD officers by January 31, 2010.	C	The first lieutenants' course was begun in September 2009.
Objective 8: Develop academic program pathways and career opportunities for DPD officers by July 31, 2010.	I	This has been put on hold. With recruitment down due to the recession, the DPD does not consider changing entry requirements to be a priority.

Goal III: Develop a national research center or think tank focused on providing the DPD with the capacity to solve complex crime problems, implement best practices in policing, and evaluate agency performance.

Objective 1: Establish the CPI executive-in-residence and scholar-in-residence programs and invite the first participant to begin in September 2009.	C	CPI has brought in several prominent police executives to help teach parts of its first lieutenants' course. Peter Johnstone has filled the role of scholar in residence. David Kunkle was recently brought on staff as the permanent police executive in residence.
Objective 2: Meet with DPD recruitment representatives to identify and implement at least three new recruiting strategies by January 31, 2010.	I	The CPI director has met with the head of personnel for the DPD. However, with hiring down, new strategies are not a current priority of the DPD.
Objective 3: Participate in at least five policy-related leadership meetings at the DPD by September 30, 2009.	C	CPI staff have attended all weekly CompStat strategy meetings. Institute personnel have also been involved in helping the department develop a vehicle-pursuit policy, reviewed the DPD's use-of-force policy, and worked with state officials on issues surrounding racial profiling.
Objective 4: Develop at least one major academic research project focusing on crime victimization or prevention practices by September 30, 2009.	I	
Objective 5: Secure funding for at least one major academic research or national demonstration project focusing on training, police best practices, recruiting, or police management practices by January 31, 2010.	I	The institute has several proposals for funding pending.
Objective 6: Review and evaluate DPD general orders by December 31, 2010.		Task is not yet due.

Goal IV: Build a stronger relationship between the DPD, UNT Dallas, UT Dallas, and the Dallas private sector.

Objective 1: Develop an executive and professional coaching program or mentoring curriculum for members within the command ranks of the DPD by January 31, 2010.	I	
Objective 2: Recruit at least four private companies to participate in DPD mentoring programs by January 31, 2010.	P	Have contacted several local companies (including Southwest Airlines and Burlington Northern Railroad) that have indicated interest in participating
Objective 3: Establish a peer resource group for leaders via the Internet to provide long-term support for DPD command staff executives by June 30, 2010.	P	An electronic bulletin board has been created for participants in the first lieutenant class to communicate and express concerns and innovations.
Objective 4: Hold at least four informational events at Dallas-area business conventions, conferences, or meetings to promote CPI objectives by September 30, 2010.		Task is not yet due.

Table 8.1—Continued

Goal or Objective	Status	Notes
Objective 5: Coordinate at least one outreach event to be held at the DPD that will focus on partnerships between the DPD and private-sector companies by September 30, 2010.		Task is not yet due.
Goal V: Showcase the city of Dallas and the DPD, enhancing national visibility in addressing issues of urban crime and policing.		
Objective 1: Begin immediately to develop a national reputation for CPI through participation in national and international conferences and writing.	P	The institute has cosponsored with the DPD its annual Crimes Against Children conference and Crimes Against Women conference. The institute contributed funds for the conferences and included information about CPI as part of conference promotional literature, and the institute director spoke at the conferences. CPI has also teamed with ILEA to hold a conference on liability management that will be held on December 11, 2010. CPI staff are also beginning to plan a conference on innovation in policing.
Objective 2: Immediately provide professional consulting services to law-enforcement and criminal-justice agencies, with a particular focus on larger police agencies in Texas.	C	The institute director has provided substantial consulting services to the City of El Paso Police Department that includes evaluation of training academy curriculum and training on liability issues. For the McKinney Police Department, the institute director has conducted a policy evaluation and staffing study.
Objective 3: Provide a venue to host international police delegates, showcasing best practices within the DPD, by January 31, 2009.	I	The institute does not yet have a venue for hosting conferences or holding classes and has to rent space. This will be the situation until UNT completes construction on a second building on the Dallas campus.
Objective 4: Disseminate research findings through the sponsorship of two professional journals by January 2009, and begin a quarterly newsletter by January 31, 2010.	C	Institute staff edit two criminal justice journals, *Police Quarterly* and *Youth Violence and Juvenile Justice*. Articles about the institute have appeared in *Police Chief* magazine and *Community Policing Dispatch*.
Objective 5: Design and build an operational website for the CPI and produce marketing brochures for the institute by September 30, 2009.	P	The brochures have been printed. Someone has been hired to design a website for the institute.
Objective 6: Complete and distribute at least two press releases detailing CPI programs and projects to local news agencies by September 30, 2009.	C	The institute has received good coverage in the local print and mass media.
Objective 7: Develop key relationships and formal linkages with other police training centers by January 31, 2010.	C	The institute has developed formal relationships with the Johns Hopkins Police Executive Leadership Program and the ILEA. The institute has also had contacts with the SMIP, John Jay's Leadership Academy, and the Southern Police Institute.
Objective 8: Host the first CPI national conference on best practices in police leadership by August 31, 2011.		Task is not yet due.
Objective 9: Develop a library on contemporary strategies in policing and police organizational development by December 31, 2011.		Task is not yet due.

NOTE: C = complete. P = partially complete. I = incomplete.

CHAPTER NINE

Conclusions of the Process Evaluation

CPI was confronted with numerous obstacles during its inaugural year. Like the institute itself, CPI's parent organization, UNT Dallas, is a fledgling institution. The new university did not have space to house the institute as was originally envisioned. This turned out to be a fortuitous occurrence because it pushed the institute closer to the everyday workings of the DPD and helped to promote its integration into the police culture. In the normal stresses and strains that occurred in the course of the new university in Dallas separating from its parent organization, CPI was sometimes caught in the middle: It was reliant on UNT in Denton for its degree-granting capabilities, grant support, and administration but clear that its natural home was in the new university created at Dallas.

While the office-space issue was quickly resolved in a positive way, the institute lacked an adequate space for its inaugural course. UNT Dallas did not yet have the physical plant to be able to host CPI classes, so the institute was forced to rent a venue to hold the classes, finding good, if remote, space at a local arboretum. The question of where to hold classes was eventually resolved when the Meadows Foundation stepped up and offered space for future institute courses at its offices.

A third obstacle for the new institute was the fact that, under budget pressure, the city withdrew its policy of reimbursing DPD officers for college credits. This removed a significant financial incentive for DPD staff to take institute classes for credit. It is likely that this decision has dampened enthusiasm among DPD officers for participating in the institute's credit-approved courses. In the long run, this will not only discourage enrollment in voluntary institute courses but also act to undercut the institute's ability to increase the proportion of DPD officers who have undergraduate and advanced degrees.

In spite of these obstacles, CPI got off to a very quick and positive start. The institute's initial course reflected best practices in police leadership training and, in some ways, broke new ground. The materials and concepts covered were on a par with high-quality leadership courses. The course material and instructional methodology developed by CPI staff make use of a blended approach combining both lecture and case-study methodologies within traditional and nontraditional classroom activities. The 240-hour CPI course template, broken into six 40-hour modules, is considerably longer than both SMIP and the FBI's Law Enforcement Executive Development Seminar. Yet, because the course is local and because it used an interrupted class design, course participants were not away from their assignments for extended periods of time. The back and forth between class time and work assignments encouraged them to try out the concepts covered in class while actually performing their duties. What makes CPI truly unusual is the fact that a large swath of the command staff within one police agency has now benefited from advanced leadership training and has the potential to think and act as a single positive force.

As we noted, the concept of a cohort of midlevel police managers brought together to bond and develop a common vocabulary and approach to leadership is unique in the world of American law enforcement. The Leadership in Police Organizations (LPO) program developed by the International Association of Chiefs of Police takes a different approach, through a concept called *dispersed leadership* (Moriarty, 2010). LPO training targets key individuals at different ranks in an organization for training, based on the belief that leadership is a quality that should be promoted throughout an organization. CPI promotes the idea of leadership throughout the organization as well but, by concentrating on one rank at a time, creates the possibility of developing strong ties and common purpose among officers within each rank.

The problem-solving and research component of CPI has also gotten off to a good start. There are strong indications that senior DPD officers understand the institute's potential and are making requests for research and evaluation projects that indicate a good appreciation of the value of evidence-based practices. The recent departure of Chief Kunkle, whose vision was instrumental in the creation of the institute, will present a test of the extent to which the institute's integration into DPD culture is independent of top DPD leadership. Nonetheless, we would be surprised if the next chief did not take advantage of the resources offered by the institute.

While DPD senior staff have been quick to appreciate the value of the institute, lack of a research director has hampered CPI's ability to respond to requests and to develop a research agenda of its own. The void in research leadership at CPI has been filled by the executive director, who has been instrumental in beginning to secure a place for CPI in the culture of the DPD.

However, as the institute matures and grows, it is clear that the executive director cannot continue to function effectively in the multiple roles of generating revenue through grant proposals and marketing, promoting external relations, developing ties with and advising senior DPD managers, developing curriculum, directing research, and consulting for other law-enforcement agencies. These functions will need to be dispersed and delegated to other staff if the institute is to continue to thrive.

The departure of Chief Kunkle will also pose a challenge to the institute. The chief was one of the main architects of the concept that became CPI and, of course, a big supporter of the institute. Any new chief likely will see the value of the institute for staff development. But a new chief may not necessarily have the same high level of commitment that Chief Kunkle has had to research and evidence-based practices. The institute director will need to educate the new chief about the value of having an internal laboratory to develop and evaluate new approaches to crime fighting and community relations. The fact that the institute director has had a long and fruitful relationship with the department and its command staff will help to ensure a smooth transition.

Finally, the institute will have to face the question of trying to identify the scope of its mission. It was conceived as a resource for the DPD, and the executive director has kept that conception clearly in mind as he has, at times, battled university forces that have not always held DPD interests paramount. News of the institute has started to spread among Texas law-enforcement agencies through word of mouth and is starting to spread among agencies around the country as a result of publications and conference presentations. With increasing frequency, agencies in the Dallas region and beyond have begun making inquiries about sending their officers to CPI courses.

Revenues from other agencies are, of course, a boon for CPI in thinking about sustainability: Capturing significant revenues from agencies outside the DPD could go a long way toward complementing the long-term commitments of key staff and office space made by the city and the two partner universities. But, as opportunities present themselves, CPI will have to ultimately decide whether it is solely a DPD entity or whether it also has a significant role to play on a regional, state, or even national level. These are significant questions with which to grapple but ones that grow from success and actualization of a concept that has the potential to truly revolutionize law-enforcement leadership training.

We hope that CFT continues its commitment to thorough ongoing evaluation of CPI. It is important for CPI and the institutions involved in the partnership to receive feedback that will enable course corrections when needed. For an investment as large and innovative as this, we believe that it is also important for CPI to get feedback on the extent to which its investment succeeded: It is this kind of feedback on its investments that, over the long run, will enable the foundation to hone its ability to make gifts that are effective in meeting its goals.

We believe that it will be key to any future evaluations to incorporate a strong set of metrics, such as those included in the evaluation plan that RAND developed for CFT. Evaluation should include an assessment of individual courses offered by the institute and how the courses affect the way that participants approach their jobs, and such an effort has been funded by CFT for the institute's inaugural course. Evaluation also ought to incorporate broad measures—such as officer job satisfaction, officer perceptions of DPD leadership, public opinion of the police, and satisfaction of citizens who have contact with the police—that gauge whether the institute affects the professionalism of Dallas policing and the safety of Dallas citizens.

References

Bayley, David H., *Policing in America: Assessment and Prospects*, Washington, D.C.: Police Foundation, February 1998.

Bradley, David, and Christine Nixon, "Ending the 'Dialogue of the Deaf': Evidence and Policing Policies and Practices—An Australian Case Study," *Police Practice and Research*, Vol. 10, No. 5–6, October 2009, pp. 423–435.

Brown, J., and I. Waters, "Professional Policing Research," *Policing*, Vol. 9, No. 4, 1993, pp. 323–334.

Davis, Robert C., *Measuring the Performance of the Dallas Police Department: 2008–2009 Results*, Santa Monica, Calif.: RAND Corporation, TR-730-UNT, 2009. As of August 11, 2010: http://www.rand.org/pubs/technical_reports/TR730/

Gladwell, Malcolm, *The Tipping Point: How Little Things Can Make a Big Difference*, Boston: Little, Brown, 2000.

International Association of Chiefs of Police, *Police Leadership in the 21st Century: Achieving and Sustaining Executive Success—Recommendations from the President's First Leadership Conference*, Alexandria, Va., May 1999.

Kouzes, James M., and Barry Z. Posner, *The Leadership Challenge: How to Get Extraordinary Things Done in Organizations*, San Francisco, Calif.: Jossey-Bass, 1987.

Linnan, Laura, and Allan Steckler, "Process Evaluation for Public Health Interventions and Research: An Overview," in Allan B. Steckler and Laura Linnan, eds., *Process Evaluation for Public Health Interventions and Research*, San Francisco, Calif.: Jossey-Bass, 2002, pp. 1–23.

Moriarty, Sean E., "The Leadership in Police Organizations Program in the Delaware State Police: Recommendations for Law Enforcement Leadership Development," *Police Chief*, May 2009, pp. 1–8. As of August 11, 2010: http://policechiefmagazine.org/magazine/index.cfm?fuseaction=display_arch&article_id=1792&issue_id=52009

Shaftoe, Henry, *Crime Prevention: Facts, Fallacies, and the Future*, New York: Palgrave Macmillan, 2004.

Skogan, Wesley G., and Kathleen Frydl, eds., *Fairness and Effectiveness in Policing: The Evidence*, Washington, D.C.: National Academies Press, 2004.